SOUL SEEDS

:: Remembering Light Language ::

Vanessa Lamorte Hartshorn, M.A.

DEDICATION

For all of the children of the Earth; we are seeds.
May we grow in Light together.

CONTENTS

ACKNOWLEDGMENTS

Writing this book has been one long integration of *everything*. It is a weaved and bound piece of my heart and soul. Behind every soul work, there is a whole soul tribe, offering support, love, guidance, encouragement, and inspiration. Here's to mine—

To my husband, Matt: My deepest gratitude for your patience, insight and love. From the beginning of this light language journey you have been my biggest supporter and a sounding board for all the things I never thought of. Our partnership has held me so beautifully and I am so thankful. I love you.

To my parents, Marisella and Angelo: Thank you for always encouraging me to walk to the beat of my own drum. I am forever grateful for your inspiration to be my authentic self and to never give up on my dreams.

To my sisters, Alexa and Victoria: How lucky I have been to incarnate in a family with not one but two best friends as siblings. You are both old, wise crones. Thank you for your sage advice and all the laughter along the way.

To my grandparents, Yolanda and Giuseppe, Arturo and Anna: All of your stories from the old country, Italy, filled me with wonder. They gave me a hunger to understand the ancient magic of this world for which I am grateful. With three of you on the other side of the veil now, I find myself still learning from your Elder ways. Nonna Anna, thank you for the nourishing, delicious food you continue to cook, which especially saved me on those days I seemed to worked tirelessly.

To my binary star sister and teacher, Nicole: Thank you for being my first light language friend on this planet. You helped me to feel safe and to make sense of the inner chaos I felt when it all first began. So much gratitude to you for your guidance on magic, energy healing and light technologies and for the empowerment to distill this book into its highest vision. Thank you for your sacred prayers of protection, inspiration, clarity and love, always, but especially during the gestation and birth of this work. Your presence, far and wide, was palpable during each stage of creation. www.nicoleadrianacasanova.com

To my soul sister, colleague and editor, Marlena: You are a true lioness. Bowing to you for your fierce, bold and strong spirit. Thank you for our late night chats and your seasoned intuitive and astrological guidance that held space for me to crack open and become the person I needed to be to even write this book. Thank you for your balance of technical meticulousness and fluid intuition. You carried me and this project when I felt blocked. www.maieutic-arts.com

To my cousins and Void & Arrow sisters: Bri, thank you for your input and feedback. Your psychology perspective is and was appreciated! Emma, thank you for your levity and playfulness during stressful times. You are such a gifted artist. Thank you for the cover and exercise illustrations in this book. Your beautiful art brings the light languages to life! www.voidandarrow.com

Thank you Great Mother and Great Father.
Thank you Shadow and thank you Light.
Thank you to all of the Great Beings of Earth.
Thank you to all of the Great Beings of the Celestial Planes.
Thank you to the Crystal People, Star People and all my etheric friends far and wide.
Thank you Sun. Thank you Moon. Thank you Stars. And, thank you to all of *you* for returning to Earth at this time.

1. INTRODUCTION

In our current age, the term light language has come to mean the ability to speak in tongues or to channel languages of the star people, the fae or other etheric beings - either through written, spoken or motioned modalities. Maybe you have come across this book because you have found yourself writing sacred secret scripts or symbols that, you know in your heart, hold immense meaning but are unintelligible to you right now. While all of this is light language, it is my hope that the journey of this book will teach you about the inner workings of the soul and what this mechanism has to offer. It is my hope that the sacred technology of this book reflects to you your own light and teaches you how to reach the secret language of the Universe through the greatest gift you have to offer this world: *you.*

When I began my journey with light language, so much came up for me: new psychic downloads, the shattering of many belief systems, and more. I am thankful for all of it. This text will take you through my personal expansion with light language and into the wisdom teachings I have received to share.

This book was written for those who have struggled to find unity through light language as well as those that have yet to incarnate with this ability. It was also written for seekers of personal truth - for those willing to be open to new perspectives and the wisdom of Mystery. As a leader in this movement, I want to say that as much as our soul language "speaks" to the Earth's wisdom of the ages, it is also very much a part of our rich galactic history and upbringing. We can view light language as a way to bridge all realms.

With the expansion of the heart happening in our collective so rapidly, it's important to examine the technology behind light language; it is important to examine the how and the why we have this tool hard-wired into our system. We work with the building blocks of light language all the time, but this may offer you a new or different perspective about it. Most importantly, reading this text may be an opportunity to get to know yourself, your heart, and your spirit on a deeper level. It may inspire something that feels more whole or real for you.

Code of Magical Ethics

This book will take you to many places should you let it. Held in your hands is the opportunity to connect with the highest distillation of Spirit through the windows of your own soul. This work is sacred. This work is important. This work is powerful. My prayer for you is:

May you see with the eyes of clarity.
May you speak with only the truest, sweetest
    words on your tongue.
May you listen with an open heart and mind.
May your heart always be full and your belly too.
May you recognize the light of your eternal being.
And may you do this work with the highest love,
    reverence and grace.

Before taking part in any magic here, be sure to hold the intention to do your work honestly and with the purest heart. Dedicate your practice to the highest good of all. You may try the following invocation or let yourself be inspired by it to create your own:

> At this time I call forth all of the Guardians of the Four Directions. I call forth Guardians of the North and Guardians of the East. Guardians of the South and Guardians of the West. I call forth all of the highest most benevolent star people, celestial beings and soul family. I call forth the highest most benevolent beings of the sky and the sea, of the wind and the waters. I call forth all of the highest most benevolent Earth beings, inner Earth beings and elementals. I call forth all of my personal guides, angels, benevolent ancestors, and guardians. May they guide me, protect me, and hold me safe in this sacred space. May they help to deliver me to the highest and purest love of this life.

Activate the text by following this sequence:

• Notice the symbol

• Using either hand, out stretch your arm in front of you and make a 'peace' sign in front of you, bringing both your index and middle fingers together. All fingers close in except these two fingers, making an '11.'

• Trace this symbol in the air over the book.

2. MY STORY

One night in November of 2013, I was reading the book, *Hands of Light*, by Barbara Ann Brennan (1988). I closed my eyes, and written on my eyelids, I saw golden symbols in a language my cognitive brain could not understand. They streamed through my inner vision from left to right like rolling credits after a movie. I quickly had the inner urge to write them all down. Seeing these golden symbols scrolled on paper elicited a feeling of excitement. It felt like a coming home.

Every day thereafter I felt myself opening up to new facets of my higher self. This experience was accompanied by massive sinus pressure and high-pitched buzzing and beeping in my ears. I came to understand that, when I felt these experiences, I needed to write. Out poured symbols that not only held feelings of familiarity, but also impressions of foreign energy - all at once. I did not know what was happening to me. My hand would just write, and I would feel this sensation of my own consciousness taking a back seat to the incoming Observer energy.

Shortly thereafter, I found myself driving my car, spontaneously speaking in a language I had never before heard on Earth. The same sensation of the Observer came in. It scared me so much that I shut it down and suppressed it. This depressed me and made me long for a place that felt like home but that I wasn't even sure truly existed! After a Reiki I attunement, I felt my energy body and physical body shifting in a way that I did not anticipate.

On the night after Christmas of that same year, I was visited by two extraterrestrial beings. I was sitting on my bed administering Reiki to my body. When I opened my eyes, these beings were standing before me, about six feet away. They looked humanoid and friendly. The woman introduced herself as Avanita. She was very tan with a slender build and stood about 5'6". She had dark, beautiful features. I would describe her as looking like the ancient Egyptians. Her hair was braided and swirled about her elongated skull. She wore a toga-like garment. The second being was a male, and he introduced himself as Farananda. He too had an elongated skull with dark, Egyptian-like features. He looked less human as his face and skull dimensions were not like that of the humans on Earth. He wore a tan colored jumpsuit that matched his skin, making him look almost nude.

Avanita told me to pause my Reiki healing and transmitted

light codes into my third eye to copy down. I quickly jotted down the shapes that I saw in my mind's eye. She mentioned that she and Farananda assisted in the building of the pyramids, specifically the engineering of the shape of each building block. She then informed me that they were from the Lyran-Sirian Council and that they resided in the sixth and seventh dimensions. At the time, I had never heard of the words 'Lyran' or 'Sirian.' I asked her, "well, what is Lyran-Sirian, and are you from Egypt?" She responded with, "no, we are Lyran and Sirian." In the moment, the only thing I could gather was that they were galactic in origin because of how their vibrations felt.

My laptop was open with the Google search engine. I cannot quite remember what I was researching before this encounter since much of what occurred before felt like a blur. I was stunned to see them. Avanita encouraged me to look up 'Lyran' and 'Sirian' on Google Images. Exact images of her and people that looked like her were shown to me, as well as Farananda. I have tried to replicate this same search, and I have yet to find the exact images from that moment. I asked her if she and Farananda were partners, and she snorted a friendly laugh, quickly stating that they were "work partners."

Next I observed the words "Light Language" being typed into the search field. I was not typing them myself, and Avanita and Farananda were still standing across from me...then, I noticed the mouse click onto the "Videos" tab. It selected the first video search. It was a YouTube video of Bryan de Flores' work. The video was the perfect resource because the first light language words in the meditation were the words I had been uttering to myself on my activating drives!

After many further interactions and visitations, Avanita, Farananda and myself developed a bond—and this bonding is how I came to practice galactic channeling. A sense of duty and deep purpose filled me. I knew I had to share my light language experiences and the information that was coming to me at such a rapid speed.

Re-cognition

Light language activated within me during a time when I was finally ready to accept my multidimensionality and own my power. Whenever I feared the unknown, my abilities became blocked and suppressed. I think it is truly fascinating that my personal evolution with light language precisely mirrored my inhibitions and readiness for expansion. It moved as I moved. In my early life, I experienced short glimpses into my abilities with light language. I remember riding my bike and singing in my personal language around age seven. When I was 16, I remember speaking in tongues in my bathroom, in secret. It came through me shortly after attending a Pentecostal service at my then-boyfriend's church. It scared me so greatly that I pretended it had not happened. More unfolded from my re-cognition...

I remember visiting a spiritual shop one day in early 2014 where a woman who was a healer came up to me and told me I needed to hold something, but that I could not look at it. The object she placed in my hand began to buzz, vibrate, and make my hand drip with sweat. I was a little apprehensive as she kept telling me not to look at it and to keep my hand closed. She led me into a back room and started speaking light language to me. Many different emotions ran through me at once. I wanted to cry, shout, laugh and move. I felt that, in some bizarre way, I was coming home. Her language intensified, and I felt a globule of energy rise from my stomach into my throat. I thought I was going to be sick from both ends. I knew what she was saying—she was telling me in my native star language to speak, to let it flow. But I kept feeling a blockage, as if my tongue were tied. Finally, something emerged within me, and I began to speak light language seamlessly and with ease. I physically felt the energy release in my throat, and my entire body returned back to homeostasis. What she placed in my hand was a moldavite stone bracelet. That was one mighty bracelet.

Fast forward to the night of May 3, 2015. I laid down after hours of research and thesis work and realized the room was full of activity. The vibratory buzz of spirits, angels, fairies, devas, star beings and outer-worldly creatures was palpable. I realized it would be impossible to sleep under these conditions, so I began claiming my space and clearing away the entities. I asked my spirit guides and the Universe to bring the astral dreaming experience that was in my highest and best interest. I also asked them to keep me safe, to protect me while I rested and embarked upon my astral journeys. I noticed the dark room become subtly illuminated by a pale, bluish light. The light appeared to be funneling through the bare, transparent window. Within seconds, a form materialized. A six foot-five, blue-skinned man stood before me. He had an elongated head, like the heads of the ancient Egyptians. His eyes were cat-like and slightly wrapped around his head. His eyebrows were thin and arched. He wore an electric blue, shimmering gown and a small, friendly smile. This man was also highly holographic and transparent. Immediately, a feeling of familiarity filled my heart. I turned on my side to face him and realized the buzz of the previous Beings left the room. A calming, placid frequency was filling the space.

Telepathically, he told me that he was a member of the Lyran-Sirian Council and that he was from the Sirius star system. His introduction was similar to my initial meeting with Avanita and Faranada, which was where the familiarity seemed to stem from. His energy felt comforting and nurturing. He asked me if I would be open to receiving assistance in relieving my anxiety and enjoying a restful sleep. He then asked if I would be accepting of energy healing. He also mentioned that he could administer a deepened healing through the Arcturus Gateway Healing Center and asked if I would like to visit this place with him. My heart knew that I could trust this galactic man, and so, I agreed.

He floated toward my bedside and placed his left hand on my third eye, then his right hand on the right side of my neck. Immediately, I felt my body soften and my inner vibration relax. It was as if he was touching me lightly and not touching me at all, simultaneously. I felt my breathing return to a steady, natural, deepened pace. I closed my eyes for a moment and noticed my light body (an energetic duplicate of my physical body) began to rise out of my physical body. Like a flash of lightning, I collapsed into a beam of golden light and felt my consciousness traveling at the speed of light through a periwinkle tunnel.

I returned to my light body form and realized that the man was beside me. We were floating through this tunnel very quickly, but time seemed to fade; the experience began to feel timeless. It was as if a gentle breeze was caressing my face, but I knew there was no air in space. I came to find this sensation was the energy of the transportation tunnel. While I was in the experience, I could also feel my kitten playing with my hair on my physical body. I was having a bilocation experience. I was in two places at once, and my consciousness, highly lucid and aware, was operating simultaneously in both spaces without disturbing one or the other.

The tunnel led to a bright treatment room. Upon entering, we passed through a veil of pure, diamond white light. I turned to him and asked if I was dying, because this looked precisely like the portals of the afterlife—something I saw often through my work as a medium with spirits who were crossing over. He reassured me that I was not dying and that we were just passing through a veil or dimension to access the Arcturus Gateway Healing Center. Once I entered, the room looked smaller than I anticipated. It was 10 feet across by 10 feet wide and 20 feet tall. The room was in the shape of a tall pyramid, and the top opened to the cosmos without a covering. At the center of the room, I saw a rectangular pool. It was surrounded by 10 Grecian, quartz crystal pillars. The man finally revealed his name: Hamuk. He mentioned that these pillars anchor in starlight for healing. The pool was filled with a sparkly, lavender, plasma-like substance. It was fluid, like thick water with the consistency of mercury. I saw this same substance when I visited the constellation Pegasus. I recognized that the technology in the Arcturus Gateway Healing Center was the same technology they worked with on the Pegasus planets.

Hamuk led me to the pool, and I walked down the steps into the healing waters. I felt myself wanting to submerge my "head," and, so, I allowed myself to sink down and relax into the pool. I did not need to worry about holding my breath because the biological mechanisms there were different. I opened my eyes while I was submerged and realized that there were helical streams of light language script or coding swirling around me. The codes and symbols were many different colors and shapes, some of which do not exist on Earth. I could hear the most angelic, heavenly music I have ever heard in my life. The music was coming from the light language swirls where sound and light paralleled each other. My "skin," or, the outer layer of my light body, recognized that it was absorbing the entire spectrum of light. In my physical body, I noticed I was "tasting the rainbow"— a very synesthetic perception.

While I was submerged, I could see 10 different members of the council standing behind each pillar. They were anchoring in different starlight frequencies from the cosmos, and each pillar changed color while they spoke different dialects of light language. I noticed that there were symbols within the electric blues, purples, pinks, and greens that flowed through the crystalline pillars. The entire experience felt like ecstasy and pure bliss. I fell asleep submerged in the pool, which felt very much like a womb space.

I woke up at 4:47 a.m. the next morning, fully in my body and in my bed. I could hear, with claircognizance, the Lyran-Sirian Council talking to me. They said I was welcome to return to this center at any time and that it was a place where healers could receive healing. I thought to myself, "wow… what just happened?" Continuing, I thought, "that was the most psychedelic and healing experience I have ever had." This story is just one of many examples of how I learned through experience that light language could alter DNA and shift Reality in the most benevolent of ways. It was a returning to home for me. The *anima lingua*, or soul language, spoke volumes to my heart and assisted me with my divine spiritual journey.

Always Shifting

Light language for me in the now is an integration of all of these past experiences. The last three years I have had several peak experiences like those detailed here. There are too many to name. Not only have I been immersed in my own process, but also I have been in a space of receiving information for how I will share and teach these remembrances. While it connects me with my cosmic, starry aspects, it is also the sacred speak of this planet and how I innately and implicitly communicate with my environment.

Light language is more than an ability or a modality for me. It is my personal lens of perception for this world, and I hold the belief that it has purpose. It can serve many. My light language is the way my vibration speaks to another vibration through unspoken transmissions between conscious beings. It is also the way I experience color, sound and the elements, which for me, displays as synesthesia. In a sound healing capacity, my light language is the way the vibrations on my voice can move or transform a space and shift someone's energy. As I evolve, my light language will evolve with me too. It is not the same that it was five years ago and five years from now, I presume it will be different as well.

3. LIGHT LANGUAGE + HEART CONNECTION

Imagine a world where we are able to convey our deepest thoughts and expressions without the blunders of language. Imagine a space where communication through love is thee way and where we really see each other heart-to-heart. Consider that there is a way for us to transmit meaning directly to our heart center without needing to get caught up in the semantics of statements. It would revolutionize the way we communicate. It would open the possibilities for expression—taking it out of the mental, cognitive layer of processing, through new centers like our emotional body, intuitive body and energetic body. Expressing our light language can accomplish this heart connection, which could be why it is resurfacing for us now. We are reaching our pinnacle of this part on the journey, and we are ready to make the transition to a heart-centered, intuitive paradigm to balance the way we perceive and experience the world. If you're reading these words now, feel into their timeliness where you stand.

Light language reminds us of our truly unified nature, and because we are all things, we have access to all that Is. We already have access to any vibration that we seek to connect with because we already are that very thing. If you aren't speaking, writing or signing light language, that is totally okay. You can experience every benefit of light language by listening to it or by viewing images of artwork or written scripts. The wisdom of light language held in this book is detailed in the Universe in many different orientations and many different wisdom traditions. This book is yet just another vehicle for expressing the same seeds of the vast cosmos.

Light language isn't glamorous or "special." Anyone trying to express this sentiment or mimic light language is not in true connection with it. Remember, if we are the Universe made manifest, then we are all things. We can have different gifts but that doesn't make any one thing more special than the next. Anytime we are trying to force ourselves to seek outside of ourselves for connection, we are simply reminded to come back to center. We are already perfect and whole.

Light Language as an Ability

Light language connects us to our personal and ancient mysteries. For ages, we have been told the stories of sacred sages and mystics that could "speak in tongues" or channel the language of the angels and the gods. As it emerges from the depths of our souls, our sacred speak pours forth to bring us into greater communion with the Divine. Spirituality comes in many forms. Light language is a way for us to access our truth from our own well-spring—our inner landscape, our soul.

What I call light language goes by many names, including speaking in tongues, glossolalia, xenolalia or soul language. Glossolalia is defined as "profuse and often emotionally charged speech that mimics coherent speech but is usually unintelligible to the listener and that is uttered in some states of religious ecstasy and in some schizophrenic states" (Merriam-Webster, 1975). Xenolalia is the speaking of earthly languages that are non-native to the speaker. The oldest belief is that light language is speaking in tongues: an angelic or spiritual language said to be channeled through various prophets across history (Hastings, 1991; Ten Boom, 2005). There are ancient mythological references to light language as well. "Some of the oldest evidence we have for glossolalia used in a religious or magical context is the babbling of the Pythia, the priestess of Delphi, in her oracles" (Dunn, 2008, p. 112). The channeled words were then translated by priests into meaningful messages.

The sounds, scripts and symbols that pour forth from us are an indication that we are on our path. This path will look different for each person. Light language shows up to tell us how we are operating as sentient and spiritual beings. One is neither more or less "ascended" should they have this ability. They are merely experiencing Spirit, the divine, or higher consciousness in a way that speaks to them.

Light language is an intuitive, heart-centered communication system. This ancient, universal system has been used throughout our home galaxies and star systems, and across time on Earth. It is coming through with renewed strength today for our remembrance. Many who listen to light language or view written scripts will feel an innate sense of knowing within them. This innate knowing happens because it is a soul language from which each soul can glean what it needs. There is beauty to be found in all of it.

Why Light Language is not Channeling

In my experience, the word 'channeling' has come with a lot of ego baggage because of how this practice has been perceived, received and promoted. What is a channel anyway? It is someone who anchors the light of higher consciousness to access wisdom. Sometimes this process of anchoring light involves consulting etheric beings, and sometimes it involves working on a higher plane of consciousness with ourselves. These are all still a part of us. If we allow it, the word 'channeling' separates us. It creates a divide between people who have awakened to their ability to connect with self/Spirit and those who are still learning. We might 'channel' a deceased loved one for healing to take place. In this experience, we may be consulting a consciousness other than our own and moving that energy into our awareness. However, when 'channeling' becomes a way for individuals to instill hierarchy, we need to be careful. While the word, 'channeling' holds a quality of something moving from the outside in, *light language is simply held within us*. It is in the water of our cells, the ancient memories of our ancestors passed down to us. It is in our DNA. We are light language. This distinction is poignant but necessary for a balanced and progressive understanding of what light language is.

Crystalline Memory

Light language is the embedded soul blueprint of all things—a light template. Our light template refers to the codes that lie dormant in the body and the DNA, until the need stirs them awake. So, how does light language exist within your body and DNA? Water and crystals. Blood and bones. As human beings, our bodies are comprised of approximately 60-75 percent water. Our DNA is cased in H_2O and our blood plasma is about 92 percent water, just in and of itself. Water has a crystalline structure, which can be observed in snowflakes or by viewing water molecules under a microscope. Water's structure is highly programmable and it holds memory. The visions, voices, music, feelings, ancient secrets, teachings and life memories...love of your ancestors and your past lives can be accessed directly through you, through your water. You just need to consciously intend to do so.

The blood in our very own veins contains approximately 0.2 milligrams of gold, a precious metal sought after by alchemists through time. Alchemical mystery teachings have been recorded in many sacred texts with the mention of turning base metals into gold. Although, in my own heart, I know that the magic of gold is not only chemical and metallic. It is also a divine, transpersonal transfiguration; the gold in our blood is what carries our Spirit. The body actually holds ancient and ancestral memory too.

Our physical bodies also contain natural crystals, namely silica and apatite. Silica is found in the form of orthosilicic acid and is naturally occurring in our bones, tendons, ligaments, kidneys, aorta and liver. It lends a hand in the healthy creation of skin, hair and nails. Quartz, amethyst, and obsidian have a natural base of silica too. Hydroxylapatite or hydroxyapatite is also naturally occurring in the bones and teeth in its mineral form, calcium apatite. Apatite is also a crystal in the geomorphic sense and comes in a range of pale green, blue and purple colors.

It comes as no surprise that our own bodies are created from such divine materials. Think about it for a moment: your body contains the very same atoms that created the planets, asteroids, comets, black holes, white holes, supernovas. You are not only created through stardust, but *you are a star.* Your skin, hair, nails, teeth and bones are all made from crystals. Your organs, especially vital ones, are crystal too. All of these important body systems are suspended in blood, which is mostly water. You are a walking, living, breathing embodiment of the divine with all the wisdom you would ever need recorded, imprinted in the technology of your physical and light body make-up. If light language is a sacred soul tongue, healing technology, alphabet, ancient civilization system—however you view it—it is undeniable that light language comes from us *because we are it.*

4. SEED SOUNDS

Mantra practice is an ancient one, and the earliest mention of mantra can be found in Vedic texts from over 5000 years old. Mantra means "revealed sound" (Saraswati).

> According to the ancient texts, mantra means a sound or a combination or sequences of sounds which develop spontaneously. These sounds were revealed to rishis and other pure beings in psychic states or in very deep meditation, when all consciousness of the self was lost and when nothing but inner light shone in front of them (Saraswati).

What is so key regarding mantras is that the power of mantra does not lie within the words themselves; the power is in the sound vibrations that the mantras make when you speak them aloud. Mantras will also create a symbol or drawing within the psyche as you chant them. Light language sounds can be seen as a mantra. The technology is the same.

The word *bija* in the Sanskrit language means "seed." In the yogic tradition, *bija* mantras are implemented to activate the pure seed sound of each chakra. When spoken aloud, the *bija* mantras allow us to tap in to the energies of each center, honing our focus and awareness of what lies there. You can practice balancing each chakra by chanting these aloud:

Lam ('Lahm') - Root
Vam ('Vahm') - Sacral
Ram ('Rahm') - Solar Plexus
Yam ('Yahm') - Heart
Ham ('Hahm') - Throat
Ksham ('Kh-'shahm) - Third Eye
Om ('Ah-om' into Silence) - Crown

Seed syllables are defined as "a fundamental vocable of which a whole music pattern arises" (Hurtak, 1987). Further, seed syllables and sounds correspond to individual geometric light codes that also are connected to a specific color frequency. *Bija* mantras and seed syllables/sounds are important to consider when talking about light language because seed syllables are the foundations of spoken languages. Seed sounds are the building blocks of our human design and understanding. They are the foundation of light language and the keys through which we access new aspects of our consciousness.

Songs, Scripts and Signs

There are three major modalities of light language: vocal light language, written symbols or scripts, and signed or physical movement. Often times, a light linguist will experience their light language in one or more ways. Some even report that before vocalizations, written scripts or symbols or signs emerge that they experience light language in their dream time.

The most widely known form of light language is the vocalized modality. Sometimes the "words" that come through sound Russian, Germanic, Tonal, Latin and/or Nordic. I have personally experienced "words" that sound Hebrew, Aramaic, Hindi and Sumerian et al. At other times the voice creates a series of hissing, clicking and buzzing sounds. One can even ignite languages from other galaxies and angelic realms. Toning is also a practice used in light language. This is known as the sustaining of one note or frequency using the voice. For example, while I was working on the sound healing album *Synesthesia,* a light language chant from the Andromedan people was given to me. The lyrics are: Sa (sah) rai (rye) cu (coo) rai (rye), meaning, "Her heaven is within her."

In addition to being a spoken language, light language is also a written and signed language. Light codes and scripts come in a variety of shapes, sizes, and styles. Light codes work in a manner similar to that of photons, in that they carry information through packets of light that we take in through our eyes. When we take in the light codes through their color and shape, we are able to absorb them into our energetic and physical bodies. You may flip to the *Calibrations* section at the end of this book for examples of different types of symbols and scripts.

The third modality of light language is signed or motioned communications. This form of light language includes mudras, hand motions, bodily and facial movement. The movement modality offers a bridge for communication between those that are able to see or hear and those that are not because the feeling of motion is more of an intuitive, creative form of expression. While a person is viewing or receiving from a movement-communicating light linguist, s/he is absorbing the energy healing and information by taking in the codes through the energy waves coming from the movement. This sensation may be similar to the feeling one may experience when watching a dancer express meaning through his or her body. Even if the recipient cannot see the motions, they can generally sense them in other ways and are still absorbing the light language.

The Subtle Realms + Telepathy

While there are three major modalities, I think it is important to consider that light language may express for you through the subtle realms. The subtle realms include the hypnagogic state (between waking and sleep), dreamtime/astral travel, meditative states and even psychedelic states. Individuals have reported seeing holographic symbol overlays in their dreams or that of an unknown language was being spoken, either by themselves or a figure, in various journeys like meditations or psychedelic experiences. Light language could also be considered a form of telepathy which can be defined as the transference of information through means outside of everyday communication (outside of speaking or writing, for example). Because light language operates based on seed sounds and their energy frequencies, we can transmit information across these sounds that are received through the heart and psychic senses. When we are signing or writing light language, it can also transmit information without needing to be vocalized, making it a form of telepathy.

These explanations of various light language modalities barely scratch the surface of what this communication technology entails. Light language is not a linear subject, so there is only so much information one may really receive through the mental layer of processing. When you engage in the exercises at the end of this book, it is my hope that you will come to understand what I mean. Light language is a deeply personal and intimate experience, felt individually.

5. A TECHNOLOGY OF OUR WAY OF BEING

Light language is medicine as vibration. It is the light-sound of all things. It is our ability to connect to the soul of all things. Light language is sound, is vibration, is frequency, is medicine. Soul language bubbles up; it expresses when we are able to speak/listen from the center of the Universe with open minds and pure hearts. It resides in all of us and expresses in the most intimate experiences—when words are not enough, when grammar and syntax fall short. It is the seed sound of all vibrations made manifest. It is fractal and it is holographic. Light language knows no bounds or limitations. It escapes time and space. It is now and it is then. It is ancient and it is new. It comes from the core of creation where all things exist and all things are happening at once. It is feminine and it is masculine. It is black and it is white. It is integration in its most whole expression.

Light language brings us the teaching of a ripening fruit. It reminds us that all things come to us in perfect timing and to pick of an unripe fruit only brings us bitter taste. Meaning, that to seek it before we have arrived to it reminds us that we are living outside ourselves. To deny it means we are detaching from what we are. It tells us that our purest gift to ourselves and our planet is our essence e n [] j o y. It reminds us that nourishment comes from the sweetness of something that is ready to give and ready to love.

Light language is sourced from the center of all things so that we can come to wholeness again. It is calibration. It is healing. It is rebirth. It is inspiration. It is memory. It is orgasm. Light language is the language of plants, animals and the mineral kingdom. It is subtle, yet ubiquitous. It is the whispers of stars and planets and the echoes of mountains and water. It is the running thread through all organic things that we have conscious access to. It is telepathic.

Light language is our refined essence, the way we speak to ether, the manifestation of our love as vibration. It is our gift to the world through our Being-ness. We all have special light languages. It is our unique sliver of light that makes up the greater rainbow of the vastness of these cosmos. In this way, we have many light languages because we are many things. Like speaking elvish, or Pleiadian…because we have spent lives in these places. We are both of them; all of them. The spoken and written languages are like keys to our DNA, our ancient memory. We access new keys when we allow ourselves to be our light.

The desire for translation comes out of the mental layer of perception. Human tendency seeks to organize, find, and create meaning. It is insightful and thrilling to make connections about our light language experiences, such as discovering our light language is a recorded earth language. However, in our current paradigm, we are in the midst of balancing the mental field with the feeling field, yet again. Getting caught up in the translation of our languages may alter our axis of truth and shift us off center. Light language is not linear. It is heart-based, feeling-based, intuitive. Light language restores the power of feeling and brings balance to our intuition. It can change the way we can experience the world and each other.

Receiving the Self

The rest of this book will be an excavation of the personal mystery that resides within each of you. The way to these teachings will emerge through the heart, your ability to feel, your connection with intuition, and your ability to listen. The information we receive from our experience is based in our perception of what we think reality is. The experience of this book will be different for each person, which is such a beautiful thing. Your unique way of experiencing the world will be the lens through which you experience the light language within yourself. There may be moments where you feel you are losing grip on the material. Come back to center. Breathe and reconnect to your heart. This book has been embedded with many layers of holographic coding, energy healing and magic. It has received the empowerments from many elders, wise ones, ancient teachers, guardians, soul family and friends. It is a living, sentient consciousness. If you feel lost or need guidance, just hold the book, close your eyes and ask your question. Allow for the answers...

For all of the exercises in this book, remember to ask that your experience be held in the highest love and purest expression of your being. Stay open to receiving information, l i g h t through all of your senses. It will be useful to have a journal to write down your experiences and anything that comes to you. Any and all information is correct. Let yourself experience the languages of each, opening you to new and divine ways of communication.

EXERCISES

Gaze into the image with soft eyes. Feel all of the particles of your body pouring into this light temple. Now feel all of your particles bouncing back to you in your current position. The energy you are feeling now is your own divine essence. How would you describe this feeling?

+Light Language of Sound+

Listen to your favorite song. How does the music evoke feelings within you? Listen for what is happening in between notes, instruments and voices.

Ground It: Bring the center of the image, four fingers width from your mouth. Exhale sharply. Listen to your breath. Do this three times. Then repeat your name seven times. Listen to the timbre in your voice. Then repeat your name another 7 times just listening for what is in the background. Open your ears to the space between sounds. What is happening for you while listening in this way? How does this experience punctuate sound in a different way?

+Light Language of Color+

Take a look around your environment. What colors catch your eye? How do they make you feel? What do these colors inspire in you?

Ground It: Stare into the center space between the three circles of color in the image. Let your eyes soften. Notice how the colors speak to one another and what new colors are created as you connect with the three primary colors. Every hue is its own distinct vibration. Let their voices speak to you.

+Light Language of Geometry+

Close your eyes. Touch the edges of this book. Acknowledge its angles, smooth facets and pointy parts. How do touching these shapes inspire you? What do you think of, feel into, or envision?

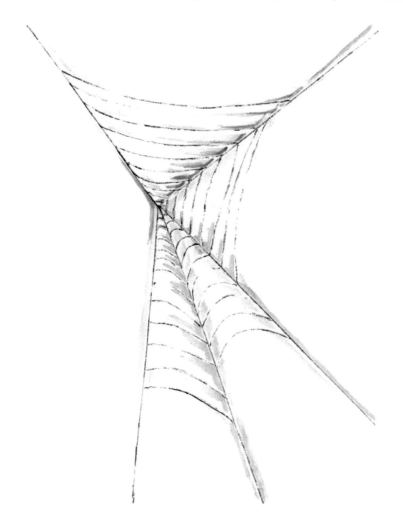

Ground It: Gazing at the cosmic spider web, let your eye fixate upon one point. Notice how you feel here. Then let your eye drift to another point. Notice the movement between points. What is the relationship? Is there a conversation happening between points?

+Light Language of Crystals+

Crystals are ancient beings. They were created through a long process here on Earth. They have much to teach us. Hold a crystal or stone of any kind. Feel its language move through your skin. Open to what it has to say by paying attention to the different sensations that may occur in your hand.

Ground It: Consider connecting with the crystals in your own body. All you have to do is intend to connect. Nothing more, nothing less. Observe what happens for you.

+Light Language of Fire+

Gaze softly at its center. Fire can create and it can destroy. Who do you think of? What comes to mind? How does it activate your body? How are you inspired to work with fire?

Ground It: Light a candle in a dimly lit room. Soak in the light with your eyes. Place a hand high over the flame. Sense its heat. Be still as you observe the flame. Check in with your spirit and your inner passion.

+Light Language of Air+

Take a deep breath connecting to the sensation of air moving through your lungs. Exhale slowly. Be still. Silent. How does air speak to you? What kinds of impressions come to you?

Ground It: Light incense and watch the plume of smoke float on air. Observe it. Sense its motion. Touch it. Inhale, then exhale steadily streaming air through the smoke. Check in with your breath and mind.

+Light Language of Water+

To connect with the light language of water, connect to the water in your blood and body. Ask the waters to work with you in the highest and best ways. Sense the water, feel its vibration. Feel your heart opening to the experience. Then, hum any tone that comes to you vibrating the water within you. Be present with that vibration. What do you feel here? What can you hear within yourself? L i s t e n to what water has to tell you. Maybe water wants to deliver you a message through visions, pictures or symbols. Stay receptive.

Ground It: Hold a glass of water between your hands and speak, "I love you" into the glass. Drink the water and observe the sensation of the water moving through your throat and permeating through your body. Check in with your heart and emotions.

+Light Language of Earth+

Sitting crossed legged, place both hands on the Earth, palms facing down. Sense her heartbeat. Feel her vibration. Listen to her stories. She'll speak to whomever is willing to listen. What shows up for you here?

Ground It: Work with percussion instruments like drums, maracas, or rattles and align the rhythm of the instrument with your heart beat. Feel this pulse all the way down to your root chakra and feet. Check in with your body.

+Light Language of Plants+

Plants belong to a network of consciousness called the Plant Realm. They each can communicate with each other as they work together. Gazing into the center of the sunflower (a flower of life symbol, among many), how do plants speak to your heart?

Ground It: Plants are also silent speakers like our animal and insect friends. Practice communicating with plants by first choosing to ask one if they'd like to work with you for this exercise. If you feel an internal 'yes,' proceed. If you feel an internal 'no,' then select another plant to ask. Once you have a go-ahead, hover your left hand over the plant or next to the plant and notice what you feel. Don't touch it, just hover. Plants speak in feelings and sometimes in pictures. What do you feel? If you have permission, touch the plant and wait for the same responses.

+Light Language of Insects+

Imagine the buzzing of a bee. Bee medicine came forth for this exercise because the humming of their wings creates the vibration of cosmic creation. Emulate their sound by hum-buzzing aloud. Notice the state of mind you access as you hum. This is the insect mind. Anytime you need to communicate to an insect (this goes for arachnids too) you can hum to access this part of your mind and send a message. How does the eye of the bee speak to you?

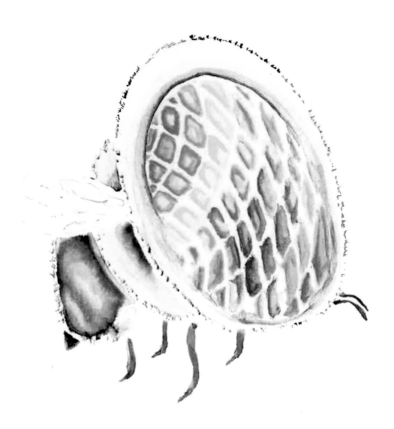

Ground It: Go outside and sit in a space where you can be comfortable. Open all of your senses to the light language of insects. Who do you hear? Notice if any specific insects come up to you.

+Light Language of Animals+

Many animals speak in different ways. Reptiles absorb frequency through their bodies. Cetaceans, like dolphins and whales, use sonar to send and receive frequencies. What all animals have in common is that they do not use a syntactical language like we do. Think of any animal at this moment. Whatever comes to mind first will be the animal guardian that would like to work with you for this exercise. Connect your heart to its heart. Practice sending love to them and notice how they send love back.

Ground It: Then hold a message or visualization in your third eye and send it their way. Listen for what they have to say back. Often times our own pets will speak to us this way but we misinterpret the signs. Have you ever wondered where you might receive the inspiration to get up and give your dog a bone? Maybe your dog sent you a telepathic vision of what they were wanting…

+Light Language of Stars+

Close your eyes and gaze into the space behind your eyelids.
Allow the stars of your inner constellations to radiate and
twinkle. Just gaze. How do you feel knowing that you are made
of stars? The very atoms in your body are the same material that
make up our cosmic bodies. If you are a star, then you know how
to communicate. What speaks to you here?

Ground It: Choose a night where the sky is clear and you can see
clearly. Gaze up at the sky. Which star catches your attention?
Since stars are conscious just like you and me, connect with them.
Remember that your gaze is powerful enough to make the
connection. Listen for their voice, feel their messages, and let
yourself open to what they might want to tell you.

+Light Language of the Silent Void+

Come into stillness... letting go of all mind chatter, external movement, and stimuli. Focus your attention on your breath. Notice the warmth emanating from the center of your body. Close your eyes and journey with your breath, into your body and auric field. Ground into the very center of your being. From here all things are possible. Listen. Not to the voice in your mind or the sounds from outside. Listen to the pulse of your vibration. Feel your entire being contracting into this single point, a lustrous pearl at the center of your Self. Listen. Receive. Magnetize.

Ground It: Close your eyes and imagine that you are the Void. Feel yourself expanding to the size of the room, then the size of your city. Expand to the size of your country, then the world. Expand beyond the world encompassing the solar system. Keep expanding. Then see your body filling with open space as you become the Void. All that ever was, is or will be is contained in this space. How does this inform your life now?

Anchor It: Now, gaze into the image with soft eyes. Feel all of the particles of your body pouring into this light temple. Then, feel all of your particles bouncing back to you in your current position. The energy you are feeling is your own divine essence in the now. How might your vibration feel different from the beginning of this journey? Can you notice any subtle changes?

6. HOW TO WORK WITH A HEALING CRISIS

As each of us awakens to our multidimensional nature, we may experience what many call a healing crisis. This is the experiencing of physical or emotional ailments due to intense spiritual work. Opening to light language can induce a healing crisis. The following is a list of symptoms that you may experience for no apparent reason other than your plugging into your spirituality. These can closely mirror symptoms of mental illness or more serious conditions that would require the assistance of a mental health and/or medical professional. It is <u>imperative</u> you do not use this list to self-diagnose a condition that would require such attention and that you are honest with yourself in seeking the help that you truly need.

- Mood Swings
- Grumpiness and intolerance to the mundane aspects of life
- Deep sadness or feelings of loneliness
- Low energy levels and motivation
- High energy levels and motivation or a rollercoaster of peaks and lows

- Insomnia, unusual sleep patterns or drowsiness
- Physical aches and pains
- Purging such as vomiting or crying
- Hives and/or other allergic reactions
- Withdrawal from friends, family and pastimes or hobbies
- Increased sensitivity to foods, noise, bright lights and groups of people
- Increased intuitive abilities
- Experiencing of vibrating, buzzing or beeping of high pitched tones in the ears
- 'Seeing' or 'Hearing' things you wouldn't normally see or hear
- Mental fog or memory loss

You may feel as if your life is destabilized or as if you are "losing it." Rest assured that you are just moving into a new state of being and opening to a new aspect of yourself. If you are experiencing any of the above, allow yourself space to relax, quiet the mind and be at peace. Honor yourself in knowing that you will come out of this and that you are just needing a little extra TLC at this time. It is also a good time to reach out to friends, family or your doctor and ask for assistance if you need it. In the case of a mental or medical emergency, dial 911 in the U.S. or consult your doctor immediately.

7. CALIBRATIONS

The Calibrations included in this book are a short collection of the many light language scripts and symbols that have poured through me over the years. As each are living works of consciousness, you can connect to their vibration for empowerment, healing, inspiration, and so forth. You may work with them just by gazing softly into the shapes or by placing a hand over the image. You may even play with hovering the image over your heart or other chakras. Let your intuition lead you.

+Higher Truth+

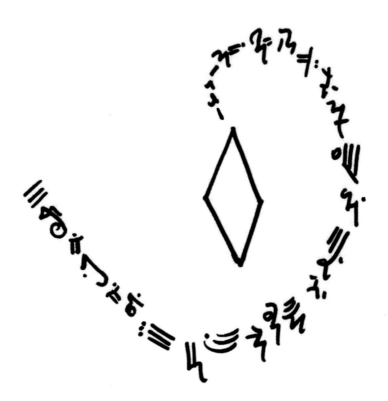

+Soul Star Activation+

VANESSA LAMORTE HARTSHORN

+Ancestral Bloodline Clearing+

+Balancing the Hemispheres+

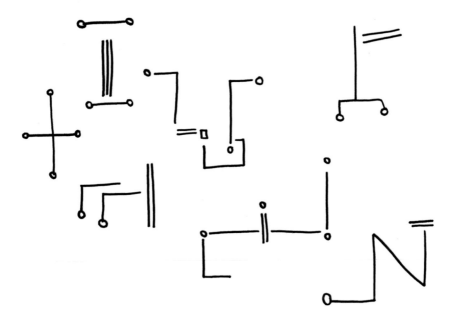

+Peace Blessings+

+Gayatri Mantra+

+Ho'oponopono+

REFERENCES

Dunn, P. (2008). *Magic, power, language, symbol: A magician's exploration of linguistics.* Woodbury, MN: Llewellyn.

Glossolalia. (2014, February 12). *Merriam-Webster.com.* https://www.merriam-webster.com

Hastings, A. (1991). *With the tongues of men and angels.* Orlando, FL: Holt, Rinehart and Winston, Inc.

Hurtak, J. J. (1977). *The book of knowledge: The keys of encoh.* Los Gatos, CA: The Academy for Future Science.

Ten Boom, C. (2005). *Answering your questions about speaking in tongues.* Grand Rapids, MI: Bethany House.

Saraswati. S. (2002). *The Sure ways for Self- Realisation.* Munghar, Bihar, India: Yoga Publications Trust / Bihar School of Yoga.

ABOUT THE AUTHOR

Vanessa Lamorte Hartshorn, M.A. is a Soul Coach, Seeress, Reiki Master Teacher and Sound Ceremonialist. Vanessa earned her Master's degree in Transpersonal Psychology at Sofia University in Palo Alto, CA. She is one of the leading pioneers in light language technology and vibrational medicine. Her sound healing work has been described as 'enchanting,' – she tends to weave an eclectic blend of sacred smudges + aromatherapy smells with ancient sounds through the use of singing bowls, harp, gong, percussion, and more. Vanessa studied classical piano, voice and violin for decades and performed in internationally recognized venues: Carnegie Hall in New York City, the Royal Academy of Music in London, and St. Paul's Covent Garden Church in London. Beyond that, she has led retreats in Tulum, Mexico and Aegina, Greece. Vanessa resides in Las Vegas, Nevada with her husband, Matt, two dogs, Kona and Draya, and two cats, Leo and Lyla.

To connect with Vanessa for soul work, trainings, and retreats, visit www.vanessalamorte.com .

+Self-Portait+

For sacred songs and magic…
https://www.vanessalamorte.com/soulseedsportal

15881874R00043

Made in the USA
Lexington, KY
13 November 2018